Tony Kitt

The Magic Phlute

SurVision Books

First published in 2019 by
SurVision Books
Dublin, Ireland
Reggio di Calabria, Italy
www.survisionmagazine.com/books.htm

Copyright © Tony Kitt, 2019

Cover image © Glenda Torrado, 2019

Design © SurVision Books, 2019

ISBN: 978-1-912963-08-9

This book is in copyright. No part of this publication may be reproduced, stored in a retrieval system, or transmitted in any form or by any means without the prior permission in writing from the publisher.

CONTENTS

Phlutissimo	5
Papageno and Imperial Eagle	6
Serving His Country	8
The Appearance of Prof. Sarastro before the People	10
Togetherness	11
Tamino, Panina and Poetry	12
Labyrinth	14
The Phantom of Hunger	16
Forces of Nature	18
The Temple of Nature	19
The Great Stone Face	20
Tamino's Trial of Wisdom	21
The Ghost and an Idyll	22
Papageno and the Wall	24
The Temple of Knowledge	26
The Temple of Reason	28
The Temple of Ordeal	30
The Future	31

Acknowledgement

Some of the characters are loosely based on the personages of Mozart's opera *Die Zauberflöte* (*The Magic Flute*; libretto by Emanuel Schikaneder.)

Phlutissimo

The magic phlute is made from unihorn corn
It has a piercing ability, and splits
sounds from non-sounds

When Tamino plays it, cloud beasts romp
and the world echoes
with *Rondo for Piccolo Mondo*

A soundcracker soldier would dance all night
and then sleep in the ticket office
guarding the phlute

Talk about *perpetuum mobile*
Talk about Natalie Portman as a crackling swan
Watch a sparrow carrying a swan's feather to his nest

When the phlute is idle
advance your ear towards it –
and you will hear the faintest whisper:

A conception bears fruit
a misconception sheds
twinkling mischief

Papageno and Imperial Eagle

Papageno lives under the winged shadow
of Imperial Eagle
He has a feathered soul
and a padlock over his ideas

Oh Eagle, what big claws you have! says Papageno
And your beak is greater than the shape of my confidence!

Worm, says Imperial Eagle

Do you perceive me as a worm? says Papageno

Worm, worm, worm, says Imperial Eagle

*Ah, what a strange thought that you think towards me!
I've made a little clay sculpture of you
and it resembles the dove of peace*

Worm, says Imperial Eagle

*The mode of your declaration
is so depressing,* says Papageno

Pressing, says Imperial Eagle

Indeed you are, says Papageno
*You're perched on my shoulders
and your autocratic weight squeezes the breath out of me*

Worm, says Imperial Eagle

He meant to say warm, remarks Prof. Sarastro
The eagle is nice and cosy, you should rejoice in that
Your permissiveness has pejorative connotations
and this is regrettable
Never mind those whose weight you carry

Serving His Country

What is this coming together
of spectacles and ties? says Papageno

It is a bird-catchers' convention, says a cat(cher)

Do they really dress like that
when they go about their business? says Papageno
and goes bird-catching in his feathery sweater

Down by the kingdomline of boredom
the cage behind his back fills with bickering birds

It's time to serve your country, says Imperial Eagle
He looks like a pheasant astronaut
he's got electric law eyes

And who do you think I serve now? says Papageno

You serve all and sundry, and this doesn't count, says
Prof. Sarastro

Some words are swords, says Papageno

Here's your uniform, says Imperial Eagle
The enemies will approach from there
Do not let them pass

Imperial Eagle is weary
after conducting all the local orchestras
in one day
He flies off to patrol the valleys of absentia

Papageno mounts guard, as best he can
He climbs atop the limit to perception
but still sees no enemies

Stille Nacht, twit-tweet the birds

Darkness perches on the hilltops
the sky gets decorated with the insignia of stars
Papageno tucks in leaving his birds on guard

In the morning he discovers that the enemies did come
and steal a piece of his beloved country

The Appearance of Prof. Sarastro before the People

Prof. Sarastro is know-how
(a printer friendly page)

He is not like any other professor
he is more like a caliginous cloud with a silver lining
His face, a rude circuit

He has absorbed all knowledge about feelings
but his feelings have always denied
being acquainted with knowledge

Observing eddies behind the weir, he
announces solemnly:

I think of the water's ordeal
of its screams and moans
And please don't say unto me
that it gives us light and heat

Togetherness

Papageno walks out of the woods
and comes unto his own

How alone is a man in the woods? he says

Strive for togetherness, says Prof. Sarastro
You're part of the species, aren't you?

*I step out into togetherness
but struggle to keep togetherness together,* says Papageno

I knew it, says Monostatos
a thinker of a bad infinite

This is called atrophomorphism, says Prof. Sarastro

Look at me: my body is a theatre of muscles, says Monostatos
And I don't wear feathers to cover it

Man needs his plumage, says Papageno

Bird needs his plumage, says Papageno's parrot

Bird. And another bird, says the cat

*Your systems of deduction, cat, are not burdened
by empirical evidence,* says Prof. Sarastro

Papageno walks back into the woods

Tamino, Panina and Poetry

Tamino is a tame prince
he resides inside the absence of language

This doesn't stop him from writing long odes
to Pamina's elder sister, Panina

His day-long shadow gets jittery, especially
while interviewing him
It is very concerned about what kind of illumination
he deserves at a particular moment

Do you write as a man? says Don Patch, a journalist

I don't try to write as a man, says Tamino

Do you write as a prince? says Don't Patch
a shadow journalist

He writes like a king, says Panina
Tamino's poems are the finest ever written

Next month she appears on the *Blowing into the Phlute* show
Tamino is a fine poet, she says, *but there are
other poets, as well*

In three months' time, she says to the three ladies
of the public service:
Tamino has a number of good poems

Tamino is discomposed by that
his design gets undesigned
his chart of disillusion undersigned

For a while, he turns into Prince Distamino
but then remembers that there are
other young ladies, as well

Labyrinth

Tamino majored in escaping from reality
and roomed with the Mountains of Moreover

One vertebraeindifferent day he encounters
the Serpent
who looks like a long chain of command

Tamino flees to career fields
where shadows read people
Having got lost there, he inadvertently walks
into a labyrinth

The stench, the geometry of heartbeat
the roots of speech...

Tamino proceeds straight ahead –
and at once comes out the other side
into media sight

That's too easy, says Tamino
Or is it an affirmation of being?

*I'd rather you were logical
and not epistemological,* says Prof. Sarastro

Tamino goes back into the labyrinth
and labours straight through it again

Most peculiar, he muses

Are you endurantist or perdurantist? says Prof. Sarastro

*Was it a real labyrinth or the maze
of your inner thoughts?* says Pamina

Was there a flow of time inside? says Monostatos

A flow of conjectures envelopes them all
Tamino nearly drowns in a spill
of concrete definitions
but Prof. Sarastro catches him with the arcane of nature
and drags him ashore

Having pulled himself together, Tamino
again begins to resemble a black dot
on the white page of the day

The Phantom of Hunger

In the Land of Milk and Honey
the Sun presents its hungry eye
but there's nothing edible in sight

The towering Temple of Idiotism
looks like an inverted chasm

Overhead, Imperial Eagle—
a milk-white creature with a half-human face—
soars in translucent streams of hot air

He is never wrong
He occasionally calls Tamino
with a honeyed song

Enter the Phantom of Hunger
a pale puffy fellow with washy eyes

He tells lies
He tries to dematerialise
provisions from Tamino's rucksack
He tries to dematerialise the Alps

*Have you ever shared a crust of bread
with a living soul?* says Tamino

The Phantom of Hunger instantly turns
into a blind and deaf spot

Next morning his silhouette shows itself one-dimensionally
and rather intentionally
against the colourless background of the annual budget

Forces of Nature

Nature makes Tamino a qua proposition
which is rather optical

Tamino's reply is musical

*Is it Tamino playing a qua flute
or qua Tamino playing the magic phlute?*
says Prof. Sarastro

Tamino surveys the world with his moony eyes
and then settles among the tribe
dwelling on the slope of a volcano

What am I? he asks himself
Am I my pain? Am I my brain?

Do you know the balancings of the clouds? says Prof. Sarastro
from between the clouds

Loosely knitted cloudlets travel up and down Tamino's body
He enjoys warm bed buddies
and hot breakfasts

The volcano is pleased with the human presence

It occasionally dines with tornadoes, floods and epidemics
and one can read in its weatherworn face:
you butchers!

The Temple of Nature

In the Temple of Nature, there are
warriors among priests
and priests among scientists

Beyond the temple walls, pink plastic babies
make their way through the thicket
all in one direction

Over their heads, a golden arrow glares in the sky
as well as bright images of Darwin and T. H. Huxley

An enormous brown ape sits there propping a tree
and peeling an orange
Little black monkeys queue within range
to scratch his heels

If another great ape appears nearby, he walks
straight through the first ape's form
without causing him the slightest harm

The mighty exist in different worlds, says Prof. Sarastro

Like a young man and his role model, says Tamino

Like a human form and every other hurricane,
says the wind

The Great Stone Face

Tamino is a living man in a non-living space
he is wildly tolerant of human presence

There's too much sky in my eyes, he says

The Eye in the Sky reduces its brightness

Tamino looks up and notices the Great Stone Face
high up in the Alps

The Great Stone Face is a gigantic plaster mask
It resembles mouldy bread
It resembles a domesticated existential threat

It resembles Prof. Sarastro

Tamino squeezes behind it
and finds bats hovering in the frontal sinus
and grass snakes coiled up in the nasal cavity

Frog-infested ditchwater has risen above the mask's chin
shaping the bulging sacks of the lips

Holy fibs, says Tamino
Imagine, a slightest movement of these lips
determining the course of our lives
for many a long year

Tamino's Trial of Wisdom

*Wisdom is cold as a cloud
and even less transparent,* says Prof. Sarastro

Life is a cabinet of fog, says Monostatos

Having disembarked from a brougham
into the brouhaha of the day
Tamino uses a crow-bar to enter a long tunnel
The grey light of Graybar Land is barely visible
at the end of it

You should have already been there, grumbles a priest

Tamino contrives to get instantly
to the end of the tunnel, where he finds
a ladder

*You should have been at the top of it
by now,* hisses another priest

I am at the top of it, says Tamino
because he really is there

*You should have squeezed
through the eye of a needle,* rumbles yet another priest

Naturallement I already have, says Tamino

Nevertheless, he is late for his life
and so Monostatos begins to live it for him

The Ghost and an Idyll

Monostatos is a bureaucrustacean

Are you euphoric or logophoric? says Prof. Sarastro

I am empathic, says Monostatos
*I have sympathy for those who suffered
because of me*

What possessed you? says Tamino

*Was it the secundum quid ad simpliciter inference
or just the fallacy of limited decisions?* says Prof. Sarastro

*It was the unkindly ghost called Zhikhar
who has a scar
and comes from afar,* says Monostatos

Can anyone behold him? says Tamino

*You'll see him if you descend to the third step of the ladder
leading down to the pigsty in your basement,
lower your head to your knees
and look back between your legs,* says Monostatos

I'd rather not, says Tamino
Besides, there's no pigsty in my basement

*Peasant girls use the same method
to catch a glimpse of their future husbands,* says Pamina

But how do they distinguish a future husband from that ghost? says Tamino

Are you sure they do? says Pamina

Papageno and the Wall

Papageno kills wild beasts of his imagination
with the shadow of his little finger

One finicky morning he embarks
on a journey towards the loping future
through the walloping wall

The wall consists of broken promises, opera librettos
and bricklayers' manuals

On this side, Papageno's dog barks commands

On the other side, the three ladies of the public service
supervise the repair of foreseeable damages

As Papageno drags himself through the wall
it is being mended and cemented around him

Do you not want me here, then? says Papageno's head
to the three ladies' aprons

The aprons remain busily silent

Papageno finally gets stuck in the wall

Can you see the way forwards? says the dog
to Papageno's behind

Where is your naughty half? say the three ladies
to the protruding Papageno's torso

*You can't be on both sides
at the same time,* says Monostatos

*Quantum theory dictates that you can be in two places
at the same time,* says Prof. Sarastro

Apparently I am, says Papageno
and surrenders to four-dimensionalism

The three ladies of the public service announce
a charity initiative to feed people
stuck in the community walls

The Temple of Knowledge

Prince Tamino gets an exclusive admission
to the Temple of Knowledge
located inside Prof. Sarastro's head

It's beautiful in there: paper orchards blossom
while little ornate Cupid fountains gurgle niceties
to each other

It is stuffy in there, too

Prof. Sarastro pats on the temple wall
It is, by interpretation, a stone, he says

What am I? says Tamino

You are atoms, says Prof. Sarastro
Pamina is atoms, Monostatos is atoms
Papageno is atoms, his bird-cage is atoms
The magic phlute is atoms

What is magic then?

Magic is helium (hellion) atoms
sometimes quarks

What is music?

*Music is a vestige of atoms congruent to the circumstances
of their history, rising high up to the absence of limits
embracing their identity, morphing to lose their identity
then morphing again to re-embrace it*

And words?

*Words are collisions of atoms, their diversions
and aversions, their inner pressure
their trembling
their final non-being*

Also sprach Prof. Sarastro

The Temple of Reason

Under a magnolia tree from Mongolia
there is the entrance
guarded by two armoured men

Their teeth are icicles
their eyes bicycles
We'll protect you from yourself, the guards say

Tamino is a trial, he is allowed to enter
Pamina is an error, she is allowed to enter
through the back door

Inside, there's only one chair
and they take turns sitting in it

Prof. Sarastro is a Rubik's cube
his spleen side is his green side
his trite side is his white side
his dread side is his red side
his goo side is his blue side
he sometimes marshmallows into yellow

Worship me, says Prof. Sarastro

Don't get too biblical, says Tamino

Solve me, says Prof Sarastro

Pamina instantly solves the puzzle
using God's algorithm

Not bad, says Prof. Sarastro
*Now, what you both don't understand
is heaven
It has no development and no past –
or even future*

Pamina and Tamino zero in
on surrounding nothingness

The Temple of Ordeal

There are several façades punctuated
by multiple windows
Bad luck gets sucked in through small panes
It is called politics

At a non-extendable table
clay sculptures debate the merits (or lack thereof)
of each

When the squabbling dies down
they all except the one being discussed
pull on their liripipe hoods and vote
with their thumbs, or—lacking those—
with their toes

An unsmiling man wielding a sledgehammer
walks to and fro behind their backs
He avidly awaits
poll results
Candles amplify his shadow tenfold

Rough-edged shards of humanity
fly in all directions

The chair force is in
—in numbers—
to not confront any single body.

The Future

People are pointed –
every single Persian, says Prof. Sarastro
disguised as Gertrude Stein

As Tamino and Pamina cross the woods of aberration
Mozart borrows the magic phlute and blows into it
Nothing happens, but he somehow sees
the feet of the Bismarck monument
dancing *The Riverdance*

The future is wild and flat-footed, Mozart thinks
Music will be like a cat's tail
Love will have kitty ears
There will be outcrops of sugar across the universe
separated by rivulets of blood
No one will notice anything noticeable
Expectations will be conspicuous
so somebody will travel to Salzburg
by the train of breath
only to find himself in his Vienna lodgings
the day before writing his wedding vows
to reality

More poetry published by SurVision Books

Noelle Kocot. *Humanity*
(New Poetics: USA)
ISBN 978-1-9995903-0-7

Ciaran O'Driscoll. *The Speaking Trees*
(New Poetics: Ireland)
ISBN 978-1-9995903-1-4

Helen Ivory. *Maps of the Abandoned City*
(New Poetics: England)
ISBN 978-1-912963-04-1

Elin O'Hara Slavick. *Cameramouth*
(New Poetics: USA)
ISBN 978-1-9995903-4-5

John W. Sexton. *Inverted Night*
(New Poetics: Ireland)
ISBN 978-1-912963-05-8

Afric McGlinchey. *Invisible Insane*
(New Poetics: Ireland)
ISBN 978-1-9995903-3-8

George Kalamaras. *That Moment of Wept*
ISBN 978-1-9995903-7-6

Anton Yakovlev. *Chronos Dines Alone*
(Winner of James Tate Poetry Prize 2018)
ISBN 978-1-912963-01-0

Bob Lucky. *Conversation Starters in a Language No One Speaks*
(Winner of James Tate Poetry Prize 2018)
ISBN 978-1-912963-00-3

Christopher Prewitt. *Paradise Hammer*
(Winner of James Tate Poetry Prize 2018)
ISBN 978-1-9995903-9-0

Mikko Harvey & Jake Bauer. *Idaho Falls*
(Winner of James Tate Poetry Prize 2018)
ISBN 978-1-912963-02-7

Anatoly Kudryavitsky. *Stowaway*
(New Poetics: Ireland)
ISBN 978-1-9995903-2-1

Maria Grazia Calandrone. *Fossils*
Translated from Italian
(New Poetics: Italy)
ISBN 978-1-9995903-6-9

Sergey Biryukov. *Transformations*
Translated from Russian
(New Poetics: Russia)
ISBN 978-1-9995903-5-2

Alexander Korotko. *Irrazionalismo*
Translated from Russian
(New Poetics: Ukraine)
ISBN 978-1-912963-06-5

Anton G. Leitner. *Selected Poems 1981–2015*
Translated from German
ISBN 978-1-9995903-8-3

Tim Murphy. *The Cacti Do Not Move*
(New Poetics: Ireland)
ISBN 978-1-912963-07-2

All our books are available to order via
http://survisionmagazine.com/books.htm

www.ingramcontent.com/pod-product-compliance
Lightning Source LLC
Chambersburg PA
CBHW061314040426
42444CB00010B/2634